D1172599

ARISTOTLE

PHILOSOPHER, TEACHER, AND SCIENTIST

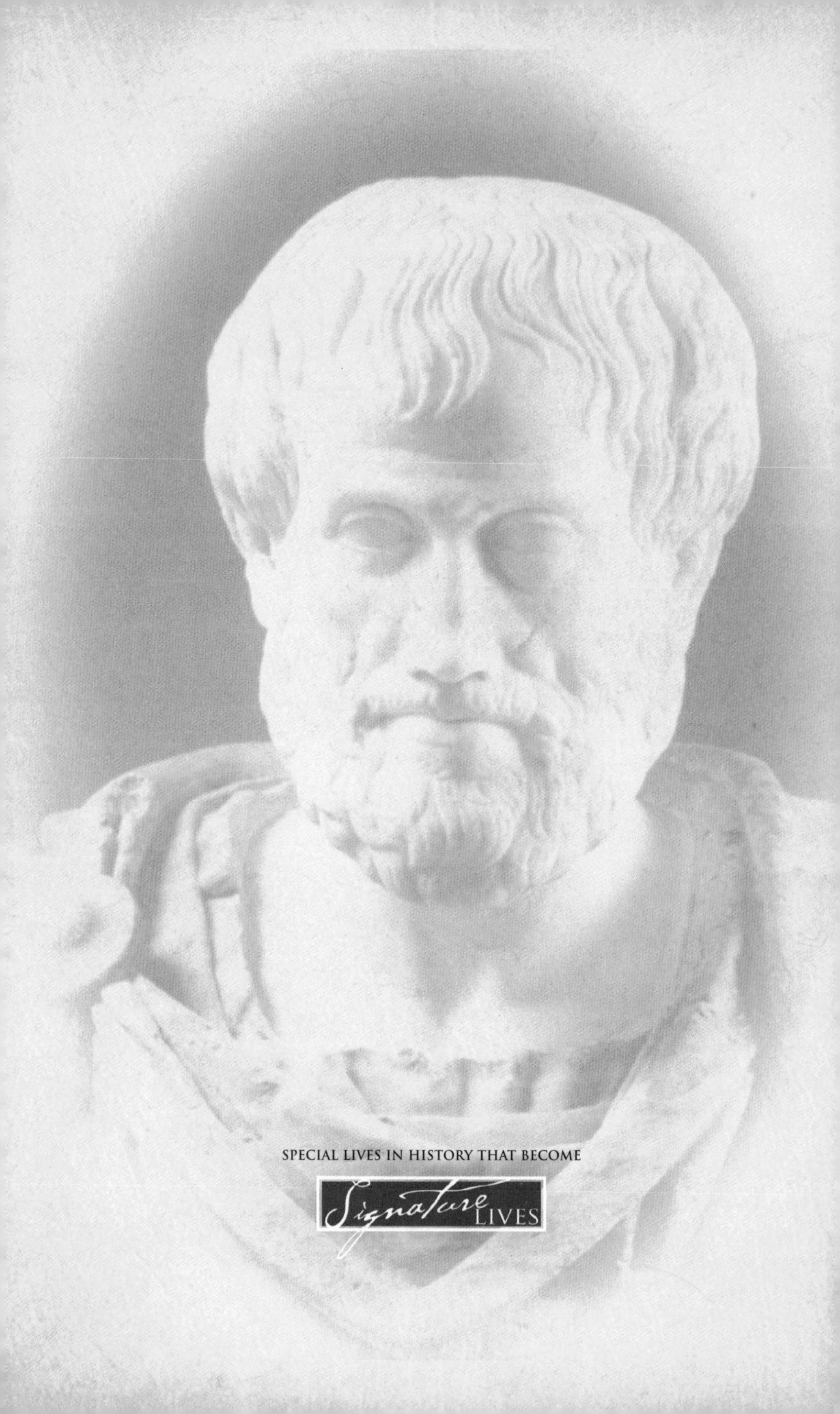
SPECIAL LIVES IN HISTORY THAT BECOME
Signature LIVES

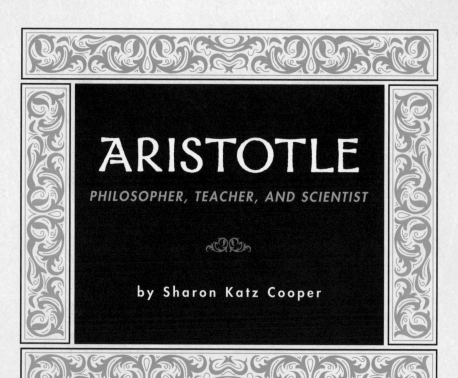

ARISTOTLE
PHILOSOPHER, TEACHER, AND SCIENTIST

by Sharon Katz Cooper

Content Advisers: Jill Gordon, Ph.D.,
Department of Philosophy,
Colby College
Victor J. Katz, Ph.D.,
Professor of Mathematics Emeritus,
University of the District of Columbia

Reading Adviser: Rosemary G. Palmer, Ph.D.,
Department of Literacy, College of Education,
Boise State University

COMPASS POINT BOOKS MINNEAPOLIS, MINNESOTA

Compass Point Books
3109 West 50th Street, #115
Minneapolis, MN 55410

Visit Compass Point Books on the Internet at *www.compasspointbooks.com*
or e-mail your request to *custserv@compasspointbooks.com*

Editor: Shelly Lyons
Page Production: Blue Tricycle
Photo Researcher: Svetlana Zhurkin
Cartographer: XNR Productions, Inc.
Library Consultant: Kathleen Baxter

Art Director: Jaime Martens
Creative Director: Keith Griffin
Editorial Director: Carol Jones
Managing Editor: Catherine Neitge

Library of Congress Cataloging-in-Publication Data
Cooper, Sharon Katz.
  Aristotle : philosopher, teacher, and scientist / by Sharon Katz Cooper.
     p. cm.—(Signature lives)
  Includes bibliographical references and index.
  ISBN-13: 978-0-7565-1873-8 (hardcover)
  ISBN-10: 0-7565-1873-3 (hardcover)
  1. Aristotle. I. Title. II. Series.
  B481.C66 2006
  185—dc22   2006005403

ANCIENT GREECE

After the fall of Troy around 1180 B.C. in the Trojan War, soldiers returned to a Greece mired in famine and economic collapse. It was a time for rebuilding. Greece underwent a political and cultural transformation 400 years after the war with the transition to independent city-states and the establishment of the Olympics. Athens became the hub for developments in architecture, art, science, and philosophy. In about 460 B.C., ancient Greece entered its golden age, one that would produce the establishment of democracy, the beginnings of university study, great strides in medicine and science, architectural advancements, and the creation of plays and epic poems that are still enjoyed today.

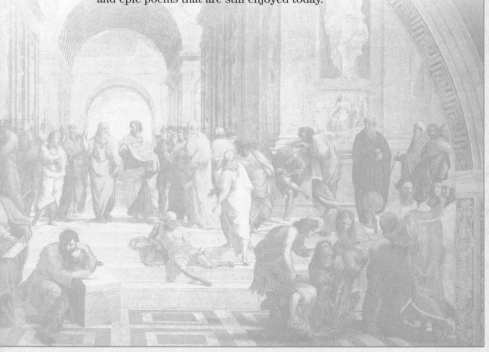

Table of Contents

1 AMONG THE TREES OF ATHENS

ec×ɔ

Wandering beneath the trees on the edge of ancient Athens, a group of students followed a tall man. He spoke to them about animals, stars, and the difference between right and wrong. The students eagerly listened as they strolled along tree-lined walkways. They were all young men from wealthy families. It was 330 B.C. They were there to learn from their teacher and the most famous philosopher of their time—Aristotle.

Aristotle encouraged them to ask questions and then answer them—using their own observations. He urged them to look, feel, smell, and touch things in their environment. He told them to repeat their observations and compare results with their classmates again and again. After a while, they might be

Aristotle was a well-known Greek philosopher and scientist. He founded his own school in 335 B.C. in Athens.

9 ᕟᕟ

A school scene was painted on an ancient Greek vase.

able to make a general statement about what they had learned. All trees have bark, for example. Or, there is only one queen bee in a hive. Over time, they could begin to understand a particular subject, like biology or physics or even politics. Over time, they could even add to what was already known.

Exploring and investigating the physical world is today called science. Several thousand years ago, the process of understanding the world and how nature works was called philosophy. To ancient Greeks, philosophy meant thinking about why and how humans came to be here. It meant searching for truth about the way the world works and how humans are a part of it. Aristotle was one of the most famous ancient Greek philosophers. He paved the way for modern-day science, philosophy, and research. Aristotle was a doctor, biologist, physicist, chemist, writer, and most certainly a thinker.

Aristotle did a lot of his own research and made his own observations. What he did best, though, was organize and classify existing information. This made the information easier to understand. As he studied each field—and he believed that all were worth studying—he recorded his thoughts and systems into written books (parchment scrolls in his time).

Many of his works have been lost over the 2,300 years since his death. Yet Aristotle left behind many works—dozens of books on various subjects. Each of these books has the same structure, no matter which subject it covers. First, he gives a complete—as far as he knew—overview of what was already known. Sometimes he had collected much of that information himself. He organized the material in a clear way. He then proposed theories and conclusions that he drew from his information. Aristotle used this same structure whether his book was about animal anatomy, systems of government, or justice.

The word philosophy comes from two Greek words: philo, meaning "love," and sophia, meaning "knowledge." So philosophy really means "love of knowledge." It is the study of thought and existence. Philosophers ask "big" questions such as, Why are we here? What is our purpose? How do we decide what is right and wrong? What does it mean for something to be true or false? Ancient Greeks were the earliest Western philosophers. Socrates is generally considered the first of these. He was Plato's teacher, and Plato was Aristotle's teacher.

Aristotle spent much of his time writing lectures for his students. He wanted to explain his own ideas and the knowledge he had gained over his lifetime of study. These lectures were never really finished. He revised them again and again as he listened to the questions his students asked and what they discussed. He once wrote:

Mine is the first step and therefore a small one, though worked out with much thought and hard labor. You, my readers or hearers of my lectures, if you think I have done as much as can fairly be expected of an initial start ... will acknowledge what I have achieved and will pardon what I have left for others to accomplish.

During Aristotle's time, ancient Athens was at the center of the Greek empire. Military conquests were happening all around Athens, and great armies were building huge empires. But Aristotle was content to teach and learn in his quiet corner of town. He was busy laying the foundations of Western thought for centuries to come. ✑

2 LIFE IN ANCIENT ATHENS

Chapter

❦

During Aristotle's lifetime, Athens was not like the modern Greek city of today. There were no cars, televisions, or computers. There weren't even bicycles. People got around mostly by walking. Horses or donkeys pulled carts full of goods through busy city streets. Only kings and other royalty rode in chariots pulled by horses.

Today, Athens is part of the country of Greece. In Aristotle's day, the country of Greece did not exist. Instead, there were city-states scattered about the area. Each city-state had a central town surrounded by villages and farms. The central town usually stood on a high place called an acropolis. City-states were independent of each other. Each had its own government. They traded goods with each other and fought

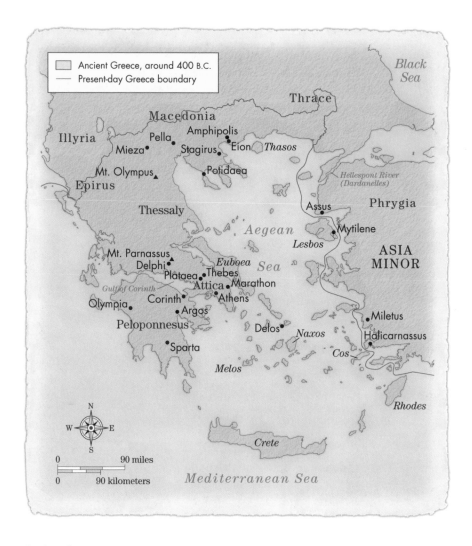

Ancient Greece, around 400 B.C.
Present-day Greece boundary

Black
Sea

Thrace

Macedonia

Illyria
Pella
Amphipolis
Mieza
Stagirus
Eion
Thasos

Mt. Olympus
Potidaea

Epirus

Hellespont River
(Dardanelles)

Thessaly
Assus
Phrygia

Aegean
Mytilene

Lesbos

Mt. Parnassus
Delphi
Euboea
Sea
Plataea
Thebes
Attica
Marathon
Gulf of Corinth
Corinth
Athens
Olympia
Argos

Peloponnesus
Delos
Naxos

Miletus

Halicarnassus

Sparta
Cos

Melos

ASIA
MINOR

Rhodes

N
W E
S

0   90 miles
0   90 kilometers

Crete

Mediterranean Sea

Ancient Greece consisted of many city-states, and its boundaries reached beyond those of modern-day Greece.

each other in battles and wars.

Athens was one of the largest and most attractive city-states in the ancient world. It had been the home of many artists and skilled craftsmen for years. These workers had built some of the world's most impressive buildings. Not only were these buildings magnificent to look at, but they were also well-built. Parts of them can still be seen today, more than 2,000 years later. The Parthenon, for example, was a huge temple with massive columns. It once held an enormous statue of Athena, the Greek goddess of wisdom, for whom the city of Athens was named.

In the center of the town was a marketplace called the agora. Farmers would gather there to sell fruits, vegetables, and grains. Around the marketplace, men gathered to discuss business and politics. Sometimes they came across a teacher and would stop to listen.

Athens was a democratic city-state. This form of government meant people were allowed to vote and elect their own leaders. The government had two parts, the Council and the Assembly. The 500 members of the Council, who were chosen by lottery, made the laws. The Assembly debated and voted on those laws. Any citizen could speak and vote at the Assembly, which met every 10 days. The meeting only took place if there were at least 6,000 people there.

But not all people took part in the Assembly. Only men were allowed to participate in politics and vote.

> *The ancient Greeks believed in a number of gods. The Titans were a group of gods who were the oldest. Titan gods were overthrown by 12 gods known as the Olympians, who were ruled by Zeus. There was also a group of lesser gods, each of whom represented different aspects of daily life, such as love, beauty, and the harvest.*

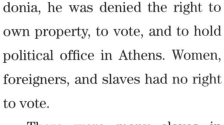

Because Aristotle was from Macedonia, he was denied the right to own property, to vote, and to hold political office in Athens. Women, foreigners, and slaves had no right to vote.

> *Most homes in Athens were small, with a courtyard in the middle and no windows. Athenian families spent most of their time outside. They ate mostly bread, wine, fruits, vegetables, and fish, eating meat only for special occasions and religious holidays.*

There were many slaves in Athens—between one-quarter and one-third of the population of the city. Many of them were prisoners captured in wars. These slaves did a lot of the work that was needed to make the city run. They built ships, dug rocks from quarries, and worked in mines. They also helped take care of individual families and homes. For the most part, they were treated well and were considered an important part of the family with whom they lived.

In addition to being banned from political participation, women usually were not taught to read and write. Instead, young girls in ancient Athens learned practical skills, like cooking, weaving, and sewing. They were taught what they would need to raise children and run a family. Women married at age 14 or 15 and spent most of their time raising children and taking care of their homes.

Boys were usually sent to elementary schools from the time they were 6 or 7 years old and were

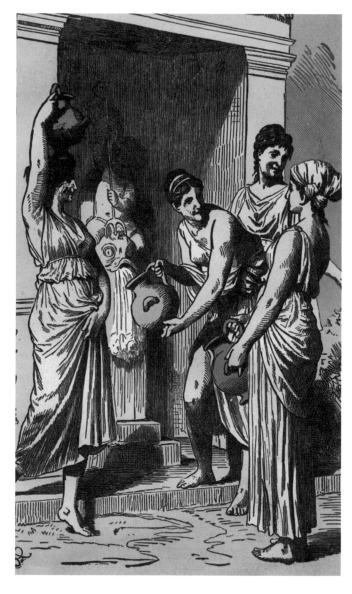

taught to read, write, sing, and play instruments. Although they also learned gymnastics, wrestling, and javelin-throwing, boys spent a lot of time studying literature. They learned Greek epic poems, such as *The Iliad* and *The Odyssey*. Greek culture was an oral culture, so traditions, laws, religion, and the arts were passed on orally. They memorized pieces of these poems and later recited them and acted them

The Greek poet Homer is believed to have written the epic poems The Iliad *and* The Odyssey.

out. They didn't have paper, so they practiced writing on tablets. By the age of 13 or 14, most boys were finished with their formal education.

Upper-class boys, however, went on to study with philosophy teachers. Athens was known as a center of Greek philosophy. Wealthy Athenian men had a lot of free time because they had money and had slaves to do their work. These men had time to pursue philosophy. They had time to discuss and debate their ideas and learn about those of others.

Athenians also made large contributions to art, architecture, literature, and science that would change the world forever. It was in Athens that Aristotle would make his mark.

The Iliad is an epic poem thought to have been written by Homer, an ancient Greek poet. It is about a legendary event that took place during the last year of the Trojan War. The story centers on Achilles, who was a war hero. Achilles was forced to choose between a short life and glory as a soldier, or a long life in a quiet and unknown corner of the country. After one of his friends was killed, he chose war against the Trojans and recognized that he would one day die, too.

3 LIFE IN THE KING'S COURT

❧❧❧

Aristotle lived more than 2,000 years ago. During that time, people did not record the details of others' lives the way they do now. There were no newspapers, magazines, or history books. As a result, it is difficult to know for certain many details about his life. Aristotle's writings and those of others who lived around the same time provide some information. Other details we can only guess from the way people in his time lived.

There are some things we do know. Aristotle was born in 384 B.C. in the small town of Stagirus, in Macedonia, part of what is now modern-day Greece. Aristotle's mother was Phaestis. Her family was quite wealthy. His father was a young doctor named Nico-machus, who traveled around the countryside, treating patients who needed care.

Before his son was born, Nicomachus had discovered in his travels that Macedonia offered better working conditions than many of the other places he visited. He began to spend more and more of his time there. Eventually, he attracted the attention of the king—Amyntas III. Amyntas appointed him as his personal court doctor, and Nicomachus moved to the beautiful capital city of Pella. It was on the Lydias River at a spot where the river widened into a broad lake. Pella was an ideal place for commerce and a perfect choice for a king to place his capital. It had

A cobbled floor and ruins at Pella were once part of the capital city of Macedonia.

plenty of water, and rivers fit for boats to carry goods back and forth. Aristotle grew up here, in the court of the king of Macedonia.

In ancient Greece, families of court doctors lived well. They had servants, slaves, and plenty of money for material things, such as food, clothing, and furniture. Aristotle's family most likely paid to have him tutored in mathematics, politics, philosophy, and logic. Young boys in the upper classes were taught how to please the Greek gods and ask them for things they needed or wanted. As the boys grew older, their parents took them to concerts, theater, and dances in outdoor amphitheaters that can still be seen in Greece today.

While in Pella, Aristotle developed a close boyhood friendship with the king's son Philip, who was the same age. His friend would shape part of his life many years later. As a boy, it is likely that Aristotle followed his father while he worked on patients. He would have learned about diet, drugs, exercise,

Education in ancient Greece differed, depending on which city-state a person lived in. For the most part, only sons of free citizens went to school. Athenians believed that men should have a proper liberal arts education in order to participate in political life, and for their own personal development. Women, slaves, and servants were not formally educated, though women sometimes had home tutors. In Sparta, by contrast, educators focused on military training. They trained girls almost solely in athletics, so that they would become healthy mothers of future soldiers.

A bas-relief from 350 B.C. showed a Greek doctor and his patient. Another doctor looked on, holding a staff with a snake coiled around it. The staff and coiled snake have become today's symbol of medicine.

and how to stop a patient from losing too much blood. He learned to apply bandages, fix dislocated bones, and make medicines to ease pain and heal wounds. By watching carefully, Aristotle learned about anatomy, biology, and the way nature works. This experience helped him to develop a sharp sense of observation, which would be an important skill for his later work.

Sons of doctors were usually expected to follow in their fathers' footsteps. Medical skills in ancient Greece were often kept secret and passed down from father to son. But for Aristotle, this was not to be. Though he may have traveled with his father as a young boy, his father died when Aristotle was only 10 years old. His mother also died while he was still a child. Proxenus, a relative of his father, took over care of the boy. Proxenus taught young Aristotle Greek rhetoric and poetry. When Aristotle was 17 years old, his guardian sent him to the Academy of Plato in Athens to continue his studies. Plato was the most famous Greek philosopher of that time. At the Academy, Aristotle could spend his days deep in thought. He could engage in conversations with his fellow students about the nature of life and the big questions of his day.

Academy students participated in dialogues to help them learn. A dialogue was a series of questions asked back and forth to stimulate thinking. Plato asked his students many questions. For example, were the things they saw and touched real? What does *real* mean? Could things exist only in our minds? Those types of questions sparked Aristotle's thinking. They led him to his many later observations of plants and animals.

Aristotle arrived at the Academy in 367 B.C. and stayed there for 20 years, first as a student, then as a teacher. Plato became not only his teacher, but also

Plato's school was named in honor of a hero of the Trojan Wars named Akademos. This is where the words academy and academic come from. These words now mean "having to do with learning and ideas." The Academy Aristotle attended was unlike schools today. It had few set lessons on practical subjects like math or languages. Instead, students were encouraged to simply think and search for understanding and truth.

Raphael's painting The School of Athens *was commissioned by the Vatican in the 16th century.*

his friend. Aristotle looked up to Plato as a mentor and absorbed many of his ideas. Plato also enjoyed teaching and learning with Aristotle because he listened and was interested in everything.

Over the years, major differences developed between Aristotle and his teacher. They had different outlooks and methods. Plato was obsessed with perfection. He always searched for the nature of ideal forms, or objects that were perfect, and their relationship to the imperfect objects of our thoughts. He didn't believe truth could be found on Earth.

Aristotle looked instead at real objects with real flaws. He asked questions about why they were the way they were.

These contrasting outlooks eventually led to different methods of searching for answers. In his search for the nature of perfection, Plato became a deep thinker who encouraged inner probing into the mind, and Aristotle became an observer. Both methods are important and necessary, but quite different. Aristotle was fascinated with the real world and had a practical mind. He was a man of common sense. While Plato was the most famous philosopher of all time, his star pupil, Aristotle, became the first real scientist.

Plato had been an inspiration to Aristotle. Even if they disagreed on some matters, Plato's ideas were important to the development of Aristotle's. Aristotle had shared with Plato a great joy in and respect for philosophy and deep thinking about the nature of existence.

The center image from The School of Athens *shows Plato's hand pointing upward, and Aristotle's close to the ground. This may symbolize Plato's search for ideas beyond this realm, and Aristotle's focus on earthly concerns.*

4 Investigating the Natural World

In 347 B.C., Aristotle left Athens to explore other lands. He took one friend, Xenocrates, with him and left for Assus, in what is now Turkey. In Assus, Hermias of Atarneus, a former Greek soldier, was working on assembling a small kingdom to match the fortune he had gained through banking. A strong and energetic man, Hermias had won control over a few villages on the slopes of Mount Ida, in northwestern Asia Minor. He then managed to convince the Persians—probably through bribes—to recognize him as a prince over this small domain. It was there that he set up the town of Assus, which was on the northwestern coast of Asia Minor.

Sometime during this period, Hermias made a visit to Plato's Academy in Athens. He was inspired

by what he saw and wanted this kind of study and discussion in his own kingdom. So he invited two students of Plato—Erastus and Coriscus—to set up a branch of the school in Assus, which would help spread Greek philosophy to his Asian lands. Plato was happy to help. He encouraged Erastus and Coriscus, telling them that Hermias should give them everything they needed in Assus. In turn, they should teach Hermias Greek philosophy. They would try to make him a philosopher-king.

Aristotle arrived with his friend to join this small branch of the Academy. His days in Assus were happy and productive ones. But the year 347 B.C. was a difficult one for Aristotle. King Philip of Macedonia, Aristotle's childhood friend, was upset by something that the people in the town of Stagirus had done, so he burned Aristotle's

> *Plato wrote about the philosopher-king as the ideal ruler. The philosopher-king would have physical training, possess the wisdom of a philosopher, and have a deep love of knowledge. He would spend years studying and learning, after which he would use his knowledge to govern wisely.*

hometown to the ground. To make matters worse, Plato died that same year. Aristotle became quite sad, and he expressed some of his feelings in writing. He described his mentor as one:

> *Who alone, or first among men revealed both in his way of life and in his formal teaching that to become good and to become happy are two sides of the same endeavor. Now, no man can ever win this praise again.*

Despite the tragedies, Aristotle did find happiness in Assus. He married Hermias' niece Pythias. Aristotle was 37 years old at the time of his marriage. There is no record of Pythias' age, but in his book *Politics*, Aristotle writes about the ideal age for marriage. He declares that this ideal age is 37 for a man and 18 for a woman. It seems likely, then, that Pythias was 18 when they married. Aristotle was very much in love with his young bride. They had a daughter together, whom they named Pythias also.

Aristotle's personal successes in Assus were more than matched by his professional ones. He began to observe nature and the natural world and record what he saw. He was involved in this work for many years. Unlike many other scholars of his time, Aristotle was

Assus was located on the northwestern coast of Asia Minor.

interested in the practical art of doing, not just thinking. To understand how animals worked, he cut open and dissected many dead animals. Most of his colleagues did not like to do this. They thought they were above getting their hands dirty. Many of them looked down their noses at experiments and real observations. They thought that studying any animals other than humans was a waste of time. Instead, they preferred to stay in their schools and think deeply in their own minds.

But Aristotle enjoyed taking animals apart. He worked carefully on the ones he dissected, looking at each organ to identify it and what it did. He developed hypotheses, tested them out with observations, and recorded what he found. By doing this kind of work, Aristotle was breaking new ground. His methods helped to form what we would now consider the scientific method.

In his later works in other fields, including astronomy and politics, Aristotle organized and described the works of others. But in his biology research, he was truly a pioneer. His work in biology was so different from what others like him were doing that he felt he needed to justify his work. He explained that it was worthy of his time and that of others:

> *If any person thinks the examination of the rest of the animal kingdom an unworthy*

task, he must hold in like disesteem the study of man. Let us not then shrink like children from the investigation of the humbler creatures. In every natural object there is something to excite our admiration. ... So we, too, must take heart and *approach the examination of every living thing without reluctance or disgust, for in everything is some part of nature, some element of beauty.*

It is clear that this work fascinated him, because Aristotle wrote four separate works on biology. These are among his most famous and lasting books: *On the Parts of Animals*, *The History of Animals*, *On Motion in Animals*, and *On the Generation of Animals*. Though it is not known exactly when he wrote these books, he did much of the research for them during the time he was in Assus and the nearby island of Lesbos.

Based on his observations, Aristotle argued that plants and animals have natural goals. Their structures and development could be understood if—and only if—these goals were understood. He wrote often of nature's "intention." If you burn a pumpkin seed, for example, you destroy its structure. But if you plant the seed, it will grow into a pumpkin. The end goal of the pumpkin seed is to make that pumpkin.

This type of argument—that there is a final cause—is called teleology. Today's scientists no longer use it. Instead of believing nature

Zoology is the study of animals. Zoologists look at many aspects of animals' lives in their research, including how animals evolve over long periods of time, and how animals and people live together in the world. These studies have helped scientists understand animal and human nature.

actually has an intention, modern science explains that most animal body structures have come about through chance events and adaptation to changes in the environment over long periods of time.

However, with his own understanding of how the world works, and with few research tools, Aristotle made many advances in zoology. In his four books on animals, he described more than 500 different species. He had a special interest in marine animals and described dozens of ocean invertebrates, such as octopuses, cuttlefish, and crabs. He so accurately described the mouths of sea urchins that they are today called Aristotle's lanterns. He wrote about this spiny, hard-shelled animal:

Sea urchins live in the ocean and are echinoderms. They are round and are covered with spiny structures that are sharp to the touch. Although these creatures look as if they do not move, their tubed feet help them move around. Their empty shells, called tests, can sometimes be found on beaches.

In reality the mouth-apparatus of the urchin is continuous from one end to the other, but to outward appearance it is not so, but looks like a horn lantern with the panes of horn left out.

Why did he use a horn lantern to describe an urchin's mouth? In ancient Greece, thin pieces of horn were used as windows on each of a lantern's sides. The horn pieces were thin enough to allow light to

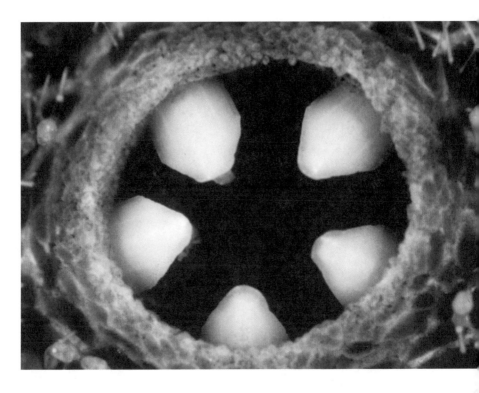

The structure of a sea urchin's mouth is made up of five teeth. This is now called Aristotle's lantern.

shine through. At the same time, they blocked the wind from blowing out a candle inside. Horn lanterns often had five sides, so he used them as an object his readers would understand.

Aristotle didn't stop with describing creatures of the sea. He was fascinated with all animals. In *The History of Animals*, he described dozens of careful observations and the conclusions he drew. He talked about what today are called adaptations, explaining that certain animal organs were best suited for the jobs that they do in the body. He figured out that whales and dolphins were different from fish, even though they also lived in the sea. He learned that cows had more than one stomach. He showed that, despite an incorrect Greek belief, hyenas were not hermaphrodites (animals that can be both male and female). There were, in fact, separate male and female hyenas. He figured out that a beehive has only one queen who rules the hive and that all other bees assist her.

Aristotle was also the first to describe a tiny tube in mammals that connects the inside of the ear to the back of the throat. This tube plays an important role in balance. The tube is named for a 16th-century scholar, Bartolomeo Eustachio. It is called the

Aristotle recognized that dolphins were different from fish. We now know dolphins are mammals.

Eustachian tube.

In addition to anatomy, Aristotle was interested in embryology—the study of how animals develop from eggs into adults. To learn about development, Aristotle set up an observation laboratory. There he incubated more than two dozen chicken eggs that were laid at the same time. He took a close look at one each day, to see what they looked like. By carefully cracking open eggs on different days, he was able to observe how the embryo inside changed over time. He saw that after three days and nights, an embryo first appeared. Next the heart appeared as a tiny speck of blood. He noticed that the heart started to beat a couple of days after that. Then he saw "a little afterwards the body is differentiated, at first very small and white. The head is clearly distinguished, and in it the eyes, swollen out to a great extent."

These observations were not improved upon for almost 2,000 years, with the work of Carl Linnaeus in the 1700s.

Aristotle's work was the best and most complete in the field of anatomy for hundreds of years after he lived. But Aristotle made dozens of mistakes as well. He wrote, for example, that some animal babies "magically" appeared from mud and water without parents. He came to this conclusion because he had no microscope to see the tiny eggs. This valuable tool had simply not yet been invented. He also wrote that

The inside of a chicken's egg containing a 10-day-old embryo

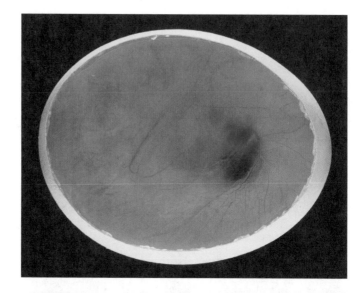

The inside of a chicken's egg containing a 21-day-old embryo

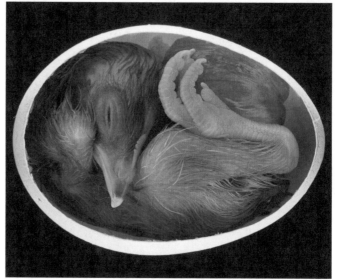

eels never breed. He thought that intelligence came from the heart, not the brain.

These were the exceptions to a truly amazing career of biological observation. Yet despite his thousands of observations and descriptions, this was not his greatest contribution. Even more valuable, Aristotle organized his information so that future biologists could easily understand it. The system he created allowed future biologists to fit their new information into a simple framework. Creation of clear systems for understanding information became what Aristotle did best.

Using his huge collection of observations, Aristotle divided animals first into two types: those with blood and those without blood. Today, these are called vertebrates and invertebrates, for the most part. His vertebrates included mammals, birds, reptiles, amphibians, fish, and whales. His invertebrates—though we know today that they do have blood—included cephalopods (like octopuses), crustaceans, insects, and shelled animals. He also included zoophytes—or plant look-alikes—such as corals and anemones. Within these groups, he classified animals by the way they lived (aquatic or land-based, for example), by their actions (predators, prey), and by their parts (anatomy).

Using these groups, Aristotle built a "ladder of life." It began at the bottom with creatures he believed reproduced without eggs, or by budding. These included zoophytes and mollusks. Next were insects, which grew from worms or grubs. On the next rung were animals that grew from eggs. These

A Greek mosaic of sea creatures included crustaceans, fish, reptiles, and birds. Above those animals were mammals, which gave birth to live young. There were several kinds of those too, including marine mammals, land mammals, and, of course, humans. Aristotle was one of the first to recognize that humans were, in fact, a part of the animal kingdom.

This ladder diagram and way of organizing animals remained more or less unchanged until Linnaeus improved upon it in the 18th century. Even when Linnaeus revised it, his work did not change the diagram's basic structure. In fact, the great scientist, Charles Darwin, later wrote, "Linnaeus and Cuvier [a French scientist] have been my two gods, though in very different ways, but they were mere schoolboys to old Aristotle."

Charles Darwin is most famous for his theories of evolution.

5 RETURN TO GREECE

Chapter

❧❦❧

In 343 B.C., Aristotle's childhood friend, King Philip II of Macedonia, was searching for a tutor for his 13-year-old son, Alexander. It would have been natural for Philip to consider Aristotle, who was a friend and one of Greece's most famous philosophers. Philip already knew that Aristotle was intellectually qualified, but was he politically qualified? Would he teach young Alexander the right kind of outlook on life?

To find out, he needed a reference. So he turned to his friend and colleague, Hermias, with whom he had a secret peace treaty. Before inviting Aristotle to his court, he asked Hermias about Aristotle's political views. Hermias would likely have told him that Aristotle believed it was the mission of Greeks alone

At King Philip's request, Aristotle taught young Alexander for three years, preparing him for his future reign as king.

47

PHILIPPVS MACEDO.

Apud Fuluium Vrsinum
in nomismate argenteo.

to rule the world. This was an outlook Aristotle would
have expressed often to Hermias. It was exactly what
Philip would have wanted for his son.

After receiving this information, Philip invited

Aristotle, then 43, to return to Macedonia and tutor Alexander. In making this choice, the king also chose a fellow Macedonian who had lived in his own court as a boy.

Aristotle accepted Philip's invitation to return to Macedonia and teach Alexander. He tutored the young boy and others in biology, astronomy, mathematics, navigation, and logic. Aristotle firmly believed in the superiority of Greeks over all other people, so he taught Alexander to conquer barbarians—anyone who did not speak Greek—and avoid mixing with them through marriage. He often used Homer, the great Greek poet and author, as a key in his teaching of Alexander. *The Iliad* became Alexander's favorite book, and he was inspired by the deeds of its main character, Achilles.

When the Persians discovered the secret peace treaty between Hermias and King Philip, they arrested Hermias and questioned him. They tortured him to death. When Aristotle, who was back in Macedonia, learned what had happened, he and his colleagues dedicated a memorial to Hermias. Aristotle wrote the inscription. He even wrote a poem in Hermias' memory, in which he expressed his admiration for his good friend and relative.

Aristotle taught Alexander for about three years in the capital city of Pella. His student was smart and studious, but before long, destiny called him away from his studies. When Alexander was 16, he was appointed co-regent of Macedonia. This meant Alexander had the responsibility of ruling Macedonia

> *Even at a young age, Alexander displayed an understanding of the logic Aristotle had taught him. One day, King Philip refused to buy a magnificent horse that was bucking and snorting wildly. Alexander challenged his father, saying that he could tame the horse if given the chance. He had noticed that the horse was merely being frightened by its own shadow. He moved the horse so it looked into the sun, no longer able to see its shadow, and the horse calmed down. By showing an attention to detail and logic, Alexander was able to earn the respect of his father.*

whenever his father was away. Upon his father's assassination, Alexander became king of Macedonia in 336. He also became one of the greatest warriors the world had ever known. By the time he was 30 years old, he had conquered and united a huge empire. Aristotle's pupil became known as Alexander the Great.

Once he was no longer needed in the Macedonian court, Aristotle returned to his birthplace of Stagirus. He brought with him his circle of friends and colleagues, including Theophrastus. He stayed there for the next four years. Little is known about what he did during that time. However, his wife, Pythias, died around this time. Aristotle's will, a document that describes what to do with a person's family and belongings upon death, stated, "Wherever they bury me, there the bones of Pythias shall be laid, in accordance with her own instructions." Pythias' bones, however, had to be laid to rest first.

After her death, Aristotle eventually found a new

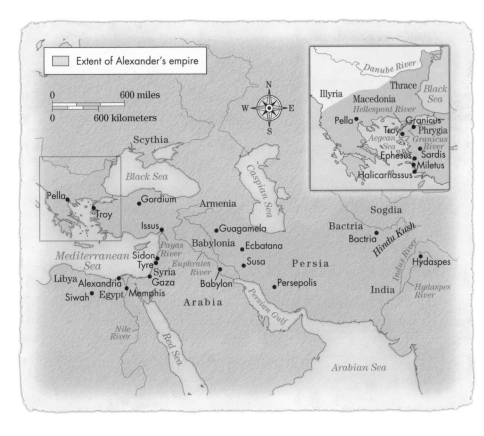

Map labels: Extent of Alexander's empire; 0 600 miles; 0 600 kilometers; N W E S; Scythia; Black Sea; Pella; Troy; Gordium; Armenia; Issus; Guagamela; Payas River; Babylonia; Ecbatana; Sogdia; Bactria; Bactria; Hindu Kush; Mediterranean Sea; Sidon; Euphrates River; Susa; Persia; Hydaspes; Tyre; Syria; Libya; Alexandria; Gaza; Babylon; Persepolis; India; Hydaspes River; Siwah; Egypt; Memphis; Arabia; Indus River; Nile River; Red Sea; Persian Gulf; Arabian Sea; Danube River; Illyria; Thrace; Black Sea; Macedonia; Hellespont River; Pella; Granicus; Troy; Phrygia; Aegean Sea; Granicus River; Ephesus; Sardis; Miletus; Halicarnassus; Caspian Sea

Alexander the Great was successful in conquering much of Persia and Greece.

partner named Herpyllis. She was from Stagirus, so it is likely that he met her during this same period. Some historians think that he never married her, but they did have a son together. They named the boy Nicomachus, after Aristotle's father. He was generous to her throughout his life and left her well cared for in his will, "in recognition of the steady affection she has shown me."

In 335 B.C., Aristotle returned once again to Athens. Rather than rejoin the Academy, he decided to

THEOPHRASTUS.

In ædibus Marchionis F de Maximis in marmore.

The Greek philosopher Theophrastus

open his own school. By this time, the Macedonians, under Alexander, had conquered much of Greece. Aristotle was a favorite of the Macedonian court.

His closest friend was Antipater, whom Alexander had left in charge of Greece when he departed for faraway battles. So Aristotle was in a good position to do whatever he chose.

He chose to open a school that would change the course of history—the Lyceum. It got its name from its location—a grove of trees just outside the city dedicated to Apollo Lyceius, the wolf god. Here Aristotle often gave lectures in the *peripatos*, or outdoor covered walkways of the building. From those walkways, his students received the nickname, "peripatetics," which means "people who walk about." Sometimes, the school was called the Peripatetic School.

When Aristotle arrived in Athens to open the school, he brought with him assistants and many teaching materials, such as books and maps. These were things Plato never needed in his Academy. In this way, the Lyceum was quite different. While Plato liked to deal with pure ideas, Aristotle was

Some scholars think that Alexander and Aristotle did not have a great relationship. Aristotle's nephew, Callisthenes, had gone on one of Alexander's journeys and been charged with treason. Alexander directed his execution. The two men also disagreed on matters of politics. Alexander was busy conquering the world and creating a huge empire. Aristotle believed in the independence of small city-states. He was disappointed that the empire was eating them up. Alexander, however, must have made Aristotle a bit happier when he rebuilt Stagirus, the philosopher's hometown.

interested in teaching with objects that his students could see, touch, and experience.

From the time he founded it, Aristotle made the Lyceum into a center for research and thought in every existing field of study. To many Greeks, there were three important sciences—philosophy, physics, and mathematics. Plato believed mathematics was an important field to study because its objects were unchanging and ideal. But for Plato, philosophy was the most important subject because it studied the nature of ideal forms. Aristotle used his time to explore philosophy as well, but also to study many other subjects and to teach on a wide range of scientific and philosophical questions.

The Lyceum developed entirely new methods of education. It focused mostly on research and teaching, not just thinking and inner reflection. The surviving works of the Academy are Plato's published dialogues. The surviving works of the Lyceum are the records of Aristotle's lectures. Many of Aristotle's works mention each other, so it seems that he was writing all of them at the same time. In other words, he constantly went

Some of Aristotle's books, as compiled by modern-day scholars, are: Logic, Physics, Meteorology, On the Soul, On Memory and Recollection, On Dreams, On Sleep and Waking, On Breath, The History of Animals, On the Parts of Animals, On Motion in Animals, On the Generation of Animals, Economics, Politics, Poetics, and Metaphysics.

RETTORICA,

ET POETICA
D'ARISTO-
TILE

Tradotte di Greco

In Lingua Vulgare Fiorentina da
Bernardo Segni Gentil'huo-
mo, & Accademico
Fiorentino.

IN FIRENZE

APPRESSO LORENZO TORRENTINO
Impreffor Ducale. :*MD XLIX.*

Con Priuilegio di Papa Pagolo III. Et Carlo V. Imp. & di
C O S I M O Duca II. di Firenze.

back and revised each lecture as he continued his research and teaching. His writings from the Lyceum are almost all works in progress.

A 1549 translation of Aristotle's Rhetoric and Poetics

A fresco of Aristotle describing the animals that Alexander sent him, from the Assemblée Nationale in Paris, France

Some historians believe that Alexander the Great, Aristotle's former pupil, did not forget him. As a ruler, he gave donations to the Lyceum and sent samples of plants, animals, and rocks from many lands he conquered. Aristotle collected them into what is believed to be the first zoo and museum.

The Lyceum was an active and popular place. Students went there to learn from the famous teacher. They went to study biology, astronomy, mathematics, physics, politics, literature, and moral values. Before they could begin to understand all of those topics, however, Aristotle had something else in mind for them. ❧

Alexander the Great may have helped Aristotle collect plants and animals.

6 THINKING ABOUT THINKING

 ❧

At the newly founded Lyceum, a student might be interested in biology or astronomy or physics. As the leader of the school, though, Aristotle did not encourage his students to start there. Before exploring those topics, Aristotle wanted his students to think about how humans could think and reason. How were people even *able* to think? How should they organize their thoughts? He wanted his students to have systems for thinking. Like shelves on a bookcase, he wanted students to have spaces in their brains to place and organize all the new thoughts they would gain.

During his many hours of exploring plants and animals, it was natural for Aristotle to think about how humans fit into the natural world he observed. This led him to think about what set people apart from other animals. He believed that people had a higher kind of soul, a rational soul. But how was the soul connected to the body?

In his work, *On the Soul*, Aristotle argued that the soul was an important part of a person—it was what made each person unique. He believed that all objects, including living organisms, were composed of a potential (their matter) and a reality (their form). A block of marble, for example, has potential to become a sculpture. A seed has the potential to grow into a living plant. He thought of the soul as the "form" of the body, and the body as the "matter" of the soul. Plants, he thought, had the lowest kind of souls. Animals had higher souls. Humans alone had rational souls. Plants were able only to find nutrients, grow, and reproduce. Animals could do all those things and also use their senses and move. People alone had the ability to reason.

To Aristotle, the soul was immortal—it never died. When a person used his "mind," the part of the soul able to think, for pure thought and became aware of itself thinking, it became a part of the divine. Then it was eternal. This theory led him to important realizations. Aristotle wrote in reference to the soul, "This alone is immortal and eternal." He believed that people should try to think beyond their material needs. They should seek knowledge and understanding. This would lead them to develop their eternal souls.

What exactly, then, was knowledge? In his book, *Metaphysics*, Aristotle described stages of knowledge. He knew that all animals had sensations, and in some animals this led to memory. Animals with memories could be trained. People got direct sensations from their senses. When a person could tell one kind of sensation from another, it could lead to memories. Experiences were made up of strings of memories.

Repeated experiences with groups of objects could lead a person to make generalizations, or general rules, about those objects. All people need to eat, for example. And those rules allowed people to reason, investigate scientifically, and produce art. Going even further, people could use their minds and reason to delve into abstract thought—to contemplate how they knew what they knew, and what it meant

An illustration on an ancient Greek vase depicted a Greek funeral. Aristotle believed the soul was immortal.

to exist. Aristotle argued that only the human soul had the ability to gather all of the sensations and experiences rushing at it from all sides and form them in these different ways.

The facts have not yet been sufficiently established. If ever they are, then credit must be given to observation rather than to theories, and to theories only in so far as they are confirmed by the observed facts.

Metaphysics can be described as a study of philosophy that deals with the nature of reality and being. This branch of philosophy includes ontology, cosmology, and epistemology. Ontology is concerned with the nature of existence, cosmology concerns the natural order of the universe, and epistemology concerns the nature of knowledge.

The next big question Aristotle tackled was what people should think *about*. In his book, *Categories*, he laid out a set of general topics of thought. The categories are names for all the ways any single thing could "be." These include substance, quantity, quality, place, time, and action. Aristotle suggested that these categories were all the questions a person could possibly ask about any particular subject. For example, one might write: There is a man (substance), alone (quantity), looking like a doctor (quality). He is in the street (place), now (time), going toward a hospital, to treat (action) a patient.

Aristotle also described what he labeled as

"predicables." The predicables were genus, differentia, property, and accident. Each predicable made up a smaller group within a larger group. For example, a thing's genus might be "plant" or "animal." Its differentia might be vertebrate, such as a snake, a monkey, or a human. The thing's property would be a group within the differentia, and the accident would be the smallest group. In the case of a person, Aristotle wrote that the genus would be animal, the differentia would be rational, the property might be two-legged, and the accident would describe this person most closely. He or she might be dark-skinned or light-skinned, tall or short, Greek-speaking or Hebrew-speaking, and so forth.

These lists begin to define what Aristotle thought was worth investigating. Once a person had these categories of thought, he or she had the tools to talk about people and objects. What came next was an effort to make general statements about them. It was here that Aristotle truly showed his genius. Though his contributions to biology were substantial, many historians argue that Aristotle's greatest achievements were in the area of logic.

Logic is a process of thinking through a problem from a starting point to a conclusion. Logic underlies the scientific process and much decision making. Scientists need to be organized, thorough, and consistent in reaching conclusions. They cannot

reach conclusions without solid reasoning. Aristotle developed a system of reaching conclusions that scientists continue to use, in different forms, to this

Aristotle spent much of his time considering the nature of existence.

day. He believed that all thinking men should study
logic before exploring any specific subject, such as
biology or astronomy. He saw logic not as a science

*Aristotle
believed that
logic would
help scientists
study subjects
like astronomy.*

itself, but as training for all scientists. Logic would give them the tools to gather new knowledge.

Aristotle called logic "analytics." In his book, *Prior Analytics*, Aristotle introduced the syllogism—a form of argument made up of two premises, or statements, and a conclusion. A syllogism is "discourse in which, certain things being stated, something other than what is stated follows of necessity from their being so." He noted that this kind of reasoning allowed a person to use something he already knew to come up with new knowledge. A thinker started with his premises. These statements were called axioms. In order to use an axiom for argument, it had to be accepted as true.

A syllogism consisted of three statements, including a major premise, a minor premise, and a conclusion. For example,

The major premise: All people like ice cream.

The minor premise: Reuven is a person.

The conclusion: Therefore, Reuven likes ice cream.

One of Aristotle's own examples was:

1) Every Greek is a person.

2) Every person is mortal.

3) Therefore, every Greek is mortal.

By putting together a series of syllogisms, a person could come up with reasonable conclusions, drawn from facts he knew. Aristotle was understandably proud of this system. This way of reasoning is today called a formal proof. Though others before him, such as a Greek mathematician named Hippocrates, had written about proofs, "It was Aristotle, however, who took the ideas developed over the centuries and first codified the principles of logical reasoning."

Though this system of arguing may sound simple, it was groundbreaking. It meant that the human mind could understand universals. In other words, a person didn't need to see all the individuals of a particular type to make some general statement about them. Anyone could use general statements that were already known to be true to understand how those statements affected other observations he made. When Aristotle spoke of science, this is what he meant—using existing knowledge in a logical way. And contrary to how we may think of it today, Aristotle included, in his definition of science, ethics, political theory, history, literary criticism, psychology, dream interpretation, and especially metaphysics (thinking about how we know what we know). Thus, he believed science to be the understanding of the universal element in the world of knowledge. The aim of all science was not just discovering new facts, but of understanding for its own sake. Delving into thinking about thinking had no goal other than pure contemplation—and that was in itself enough.

For Aristotle, thinking about thinking was an important and necessary activity.

Once his students understood these basic ideas about human thought and the meaning of knowledge and science, only then were they truly ready to investigate the world around them. They were more than eager to dive in. There was so much to explore. ❧

7 ON EARTH AND THE HEAVENS ABOVE

❧⌘❧

One of the major topics that fascinated the Greeks of Aristotle's time was the way Earth worked and how it fit in to the universe they saw around them. What was Earth made of and how did it function? What about the planets, stars, sun, and moon? Where did they come from? How were they related to Earth? How did they move, and what were they made of? These were all questions ancient Greek scholars asked.

For Aristotle, astronomy was part of physics. He thought of physics as the study of how nature works. In his systematic way, Aristotle looked first at change itself. He wrote that change had four parts. These were locomotion (a change in place), alteration (a change in quality), expansion/contraction (a change in size), and coming-to-be/passing-away (a change in substance). In this way, he separated physical and chemical changes.

Today, this distinction is important to chemistry and physics, but no one had written about it before Aristotle. He recognized that some mixtures of things could be separated out again, like a pile of sand mixed with rocks, or a bowl of different-colored stones. Some mixtures, however, could not be separated because the *substance* of the material had changed. For example, a mixture of copper and tin to make bronze, or sugar dissolved in a cup of water are mixtures that cannot easily be separated. To describe these changes, he wrote, "Chemical combination is a union of several bodies capable of such combination involving a transformation of the properties of the bodies combined."

Aristotle recognized that a change of *accidents*, such as a cold object getting hot, was not the same as a change in *properties*. Only changing properties involved change in the real substance of an object. He also thought that there must be something common to copper and both tin and bronze—something that stayed the same despite the change in substance. This "something" he called matter. He wrote that matter had no qualities itself. It had only the potential to become different substances when it was combined with different forms.

Aristotle explained that Earth had two forces and

Aristotle knew that bronze, like that used to make a vase, contained matter, as did tin and copper.

four elements. One force pulled everything down. Levity pulled everything up. The elements were earth, air, fire, and water. These elements resulted from different combinations of matter and form. Earth was cold and dry; water was cold and wet; fire was hot

> *Aristotle was right about a force that exists and pulls objects down. However, he did not connect it to the stars and planets, since he believed they operated in totally separate ways from Earth. Today, we know that everything with mass has gravity, and so it does exist outside of Earth.*

and dry; air was hot and wet. Earth and water were heavy elements, while air and fire were light ones. These elements were far from perfect. They were constantly changing.

Observing objects and systems on Earth was one thing. Describing the universe was quite another. Aristotle knew that his ideas would be guesses—because he could not closely observe heavenly bodies the way he could plants, animals, water, and fire. Even so, he drew up a detailed model of the universe to explain what he and his fellow observers could see.

Unlike the ever-changing Earth, Aristotle believed in a universe that was always the same and had always been that way. Like most ancient Greeks, he thought Earth stood still at the center of this universe. He did not think that the universe had ever changed or ever would. All changes people saw, he thought, were on cycles, so overall conditions never changed.

Aristotle believed that the universe had no beginning or end, writing:

> *It is clear then that there is neither place nor void nor time outside the heaven.*

... Hence whatever is there, is of such a nature as not to occupy any place, nor does time age it; nor is there any change in any of the things which lie beyond the outermost motion; they continue through their entire duration unalterable and unmodified, living the best and most self-sufficient lives.

It was still important to understand this unchanging universe. In his book, *On the Heavens,* he wrote about the visible universe. He argued that it was impossible for an object as large and heavy as Earth to move, so it stood still at the universe's center. The sun, moon, and planets circled Earth. They were

A German woodcut from 1480 shows Aristotle with his students.

EMPIREVM

HABITACVLVM

Drcimum Coelum · Primu Mobile

Nonū Coelum · Criſtallinum

Octauum · Firmamentū

COELV · SATVRNI

IOVIS

MARTIS

SOLIS

VENERIS

MERCVRII

LVNÆ

COELVM

DEI

ELECTORVM

OMNIVM ET

A 1539 illustration of the universe showed the continued reliance on Aristotle's four elements: earth, water, air, and fire.

each perfect spheres attached to perfect spheres of clear hard crystal. Their orbits were perfect circles. The stars were attached to their own rotating crystal sphere. The farthest sphere out belonged to God, the

Prime Mover. God controlled all the spheres.

Reflecting the influence of Plato's search for perfection, Aristotle made his model of the universe perfect. He believed that the universe was divine, so it was right that its bodies should be spheres, since that was the perfect shape. Those bodies should move in circles because a circle has no beginning and no end—it is eternal. And since the center of a rotating object is at rest, Earth itself should be at rest. Since all these heavenly bodies were perfect, they must be made of a perfect element, he reasoned—a fifth element that did not exist on Earth. This element he called "aither."

As we know today, almost everything about this system was wrong. No one in Aristotle's time realized that Earth was moving. But this theory was a reasonable attempt to explain what he saw without a telescope or any technology other than his eyes, brain, and mathematics. It took many years for scientists to begin to question this model and take it apart. Eventually, they did. Aristotle's ideas about the universe had to be carefully and slowly removed from scientific world view before modern astronomy could move forward.

... pour proffit · les especes damitie entre · amitie pour delectation · ...rsonnes e male amitie. sel · ... en tre prince et subget · Amitie en tre parens · viii. histoire · amitie en tr...

Ou premier chapitre il preuue q̃
determiner damitie appartient a
science morale

8

ON RIGHT AND WRONG

❧⁓⁓❧

Ancient Greeks were fascinated by the natural world, by astronomy and physics and biology. But studying those fields led them naturally into questions about their own place in it. If humans alone had reason, what responsibilities did this give them? How should they act toward each other? These kinds of questions led to the study of what is called ethics.

Aristotle wrote three large books on ethics: *Nichomachean Ethics*, *Eudemian Ethics*, and *Great Ethics*. He wrote that most people would define the highest good as happiness. This meant that they would choose what would make them most happy. How does someone define happiness? Aristotle said it "is an activity of the soul according to goodness in a mature person."

A French manuscript from the 15th century featured an illustration of Aristotle's six types of friendship, described in his books on ethics.

How could people achieve happiness? He believed that they needed to be educated in proper habits early in their lives. While he thought that people could make their own ethical decisions, Aristotle also believed in discipline and the rule of law. Ethics was different from science, where people could reach first principles by their own thinking. In ethics, people needed to be trained. This led to Aristotle's belief in the importance of education. In the Greece of Aristotle's time, ethics were a part of politics. That meant that law, religion, and education were all areas the state was responsible for. Aristotle wrote:

> *Youth will not receive a proper ethical training unless brought up under right laws. To live a temperate and hardy life is not the choice of most people, especially the young. Therefore their upbringing and employments should be fixed by law; what has become customary will not be painful. Speaking generally, we need laws to cover the whole of life.*

Aristotle connected ethics to politics by observing the way governments worked. He argued that only a well-run state with good laws could provide the right conditions to train its youth in those habits of ethical behavior. On the flip side, only a good philosophy could provide ideas for creating a decent

Aristotle believed the state was responsible for law. Athens had laws and tried its criminals in an open-air court called the Areopagus.

government. And only political life could provide the leisure time philosophers needed to think about those ideas. The city-state, in his view, was both the tool and the result of this highest form of society.

Aristotle wrote that while other, more primitive societies had been able to provide what people needed to survive, only well-governed political societies could make the good life possible. He believed

Some of Aristotle's writings on politics compared the constitutions of all the governments he knew. He considered good constitutions to be those describing governments of leaders working for the good of all citizens. If they worked for the good of themselves or a ruling class only, then he did not like that constitution. Following his own logic, he liked democracy. He disliked tyranny and "unrestricted" democracy.

that people reached their highest potential when they lived and worked in a city-state.

Since a city-state such as Athens was the highest kind of community, its highest purpose was to create conditions under which smart people could live philosophical lives. Who were the people willing and able to take part in these city-states? They were its citizens. Aristotle defined a citizen as a person who shared in the administration of justice and the holding of office. He believed that the good citizen was the same as the good man, and that this kind of man combined the moral wisdom of a ruler with the humble virtue of a subject.

Aristotle believed that only Greeks had the natural abilities necessary to lead, and that they alone could create ideal city-states. These abilities gave them the right to use non-Greeks as servants and slaves for work that was "beneath them." He also believed that citizenship and military service were the rights and duties of Greeks alone.

For Aristotle, it was important that city-states were small enough to be well-governed and allow all

citizens opportunities to be active in public life. He was not concerned with the empire-building that was happening around him. And he certainly believed that Greek destiny was to rule the world. He simply wanted the small cities within the empire to be places where men could live the good and philosophic life.

Aristotle believed that as Greeks took over control of the world and formed a huge empire, they would establish small cities in which they could practice philosophy. This process would lift men above the material world and allow them to share in the immortality of the gods. This, Aristotle argued, was their highest purpose. ॐ

ARISTOTELES STAGIRITA·CLAR·OLYMP·IO
Magnus Aristoteles causas exquirere rerum,
Sed quâ naturæ causa secunda patet.

9

THE IMPACT OF ARISTOTLE

After the death of Alexander the Great in 323 B.C., Athens rebelled against rule by the Macedonians. Aristotle was afraid that he might be in danger because he was a Macedonian living in Athens. To avoid a death sentence, he ran away to the island of Euboea, where he lived in a house that still belonged to his family. Shortly after he arrived there in 322, he became sick with a stomach illness and died at the age of 62.

Though there are many sculptures of Aristotle in libraries and universities, they were all created long after he lived. These works are based on the artists' imagination. Only one description of what Aristotle looked like exists today. Even that description was written around 500 years after he lived, so it may not

Artists have tried to create likenesses of Aristotle, but it is impossible to know if they are accurate.

be accurate. He "spoke with a lisp ... his calves were slender, ... his eyes small, and he was conspicuous by his attire, his rings, and the cut of his hair." He was known for dressing in only the finest clothing and sandals. He wore rings on his fingers.

Though he was a scholar and enjoyed thinking and analyzing, Aristotle was also remembered as a sensitive man. Stories of his personality painted a picture of a kind, warm husband, father, and friend. His will described his happiness with family life. When he died, he left generous amounts of money and property to his children and servants.

After his death, the spirit of Aristotle lived on for centuries. The Lyceum continued to be an active school under the leadership of his longtime friend, Theophrastus. It continued in Athens until the Macedonian dynasty decided to move the academic center of the empire to Alexandria, Egypt.

Theophrastus took control over the Lyceum after Aristotle's death.

Aristotle's surviving writings make up 30 volumes and fill more than 2,000 printed pages. They represent only a fragment of about 170 works he wrote during his lifetime. These works are divided into two major groups. The first group consists of those that were published by Aristotle in dialogue or other form that he meant

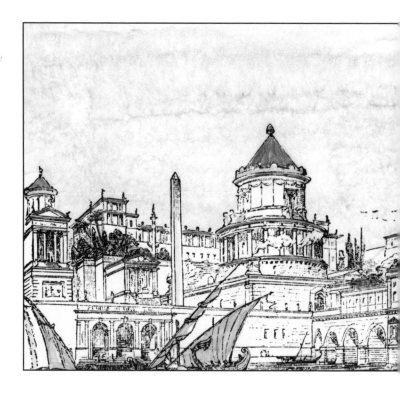

for general public reading. The second group are works that were never intended for publication but are just groups of notes and collections—most likely his lecture notes. Only fragments of his dialogues survived, but several volumes of his lecture notes exist even today.

What happened to Aristotle's actual manuscripts? One story says that after Aristotle's death, Theophrastus inherited his manuscripts and then left them to Neleus, the son of his colleague Coriscus, from Assus. Neleus kept the writings in his family home in Scepsis, near Assus. Several decades

passed, and Neleus' descendents hid them in the cellar so others would not find them. The writings stayed there until about 100 B.C., when they were sold to a bookseller from Athens named Ampelicon. He tried to make a book of the collected writings at that time. In 86 B.C., the Roman general Sulla captured Athens and took the writings with him to Rome. It was there that scholars attempted to edit and assemble all of Aristotle's writings into a scholarly collection.

Aristotle's influence cannot be limited to his writings, for his ideas affected hundreds of his students and their students for generations. Many of

Lucius Cornelius Sulla was a Roman general and statesman.

SYLLA.

these students wrote books and articles upon which others depended. So his ideas stretched throughout the centuries. The Lyceum, which Aristotle founded and guided, was also copied and reconstructed in numerous schools after his death. All three branches of knowledge—philosophy, scholarship, and science—contain the influence of the Lyceum to this day.

In the later Middle Ages, Aristotle's work was rediscovered, and reintroduced by Arab scholars, who had translated and commented on the texts. Many other medieval scholars studied these translations and eagerly adopted Aristotle's views. Those who followed his writings called him The Philosopher, or "the master of those who know." They accepted every word he wrote that did not contradict the Bible. As these scholars combined his works with Christian beliefs, Aristotelian philosophy became shaped into a system called Scholasticism, which became a Christian philosophy.

Maimonides, who wrote in Arabic, reconciled Jewish theology with the philosophy of Aristotle in his book, *Guide for the Perplexed.* Ironically, several scientific

Scholasticism was the main philosophy in medieval universities from around 1000 to 1400. The word scholasticism comes from the Latin meaning "that which belongs to the school." Scholastics believed that there could be no contradiction between the truths that were revealed by God and the scientific and philosophical discoveries of the human mind. Scholastics would carefully read a chosen text, such as Aristotle's works or the Bible, and ask many critical questions about it. They tried to take it apart and remove any contradictions through philosophical analysis and logical argument. Eventually, they succeeded.

The Jewish philosopher Maimonides supported Aristotle's philosophy in his book Guide for the Perplexed.

discoveries in the Middle Ages and Renaissance period were criticized only because they could not be found in Aristotle's work.

Until early in the 1600s, Western culture was essentially Aristotelian, and even after the many scientific discoveries that followed, many of Aristotle's ideas remained essential parts of Western thinking. The era of modern science couldn't happen until Aristotle's "spell was broken." Once worldwide exploration began, and his view of the universe was challenged and disproved, he was no longer considered the authority of all knowledge.

Aristotle is probably the one person most responsible for the greatest change in the way humans think and analyze. Many historians believe that he accomplished a true revolution in thought that is an essential part of the history of humankind. Though modern scientists do not turn to Aristotle for answers in the natural sciences anymore, his insights into the nature of human existence, ethics, human psychology, and the arts remain a significant influence on

modern thinking, despite the thousands of years that have passed since he wrote them down. He has been described as the "founder of scientific philosophy."

Aristotle is still considered to be one of the great philosophers and scientists of all time.

He was a great gatherer of facts, both in nature and in the workings of people. But even more important, he organized those facts and made them easier for others to understand. He believed that knowledge was more than just a jumble of facts; it was found in interpreting and organizing those facts.

Aristotle was not always right, but considering how few tools he had, he made amazing strides in almost every field he examined. His contributions to the way we think about biology, physics, astronomy, and especially thinking itself laid the foundations upon which thousands of scientists and philosophers would stand. ℘

ARISTOTLE'S LIFE

384 B.C.

Aristotle is born in Stagirus, in Macedonia

374 B.C.

Aristotle's father dies

375 B.C.

388 B.C.

Plato, a student of Socrates, establishes the Academy in Athens, the first university

377 B.C.

Hippocrates, known as the father of medicine, dies; he gave the world the Hippocratic Oath, a code of ethics for doctors

WORLD EVENTS

367 B.C.

Sent to the Academy
of Plato in Athens

359 B.C.

Philip becomes king
of Macedonia

360 B.C.

371 B.C.

Thebes defeats
Sparta at Leuctra

356 B.C.

The temple of Delphi,
the Greeks' holiest
shrine, is destroyed in
the Sacred War

ARISTOTLE'S LIFE

347 B.C.
Aristotle leaves
Athens

347–344 B.C.
Lives in Assus;
marries Pythias

350 B.C.

353 B.C.

A tomb built for King
Mausolus in south-
west Turkey is one
of the seven wonders
of the ancient world;
the king's name is the
origin of the word
mausoleum

347 B.C.

The great
philosopher
Plato dies

WORLD EVENTS

344 B.C.

Lives in Lesbos; does biological research

343–340 B.C.

Tutors Alexander in Pella, Macedonia

345 B.C.

345 B.C.

Hermias, the ruler of Assus, is captured and killed by the Persians

338 B.C.

Macedonian army defeats Athens; the League of Corinth is founded

ARISTOTLE'S LIFE

335 B.C.

Aristotle opens the
Lyceum in Athens

335 B.C.

336 B.C.

Philip II is assas-
sinated and his son,
Alexander the Great,
becomes king
of Macedonia

334 B.C.

Alexander the Great
begins his war
against Persia

WORLD EVENTS

322 B.C.

To avoid a death sentence, Aristotle leaves for Euboea and dies shortly after arriving

325 B.C.

Greek explorer Pytheas of Massilia (present-day Marseille, France) makes the first recorded visit by a Greek to what is now Great Britain

323 B.C.

Alexander the Great dies in Babylon and his successors begin to carve up his empire

DATE OF BIRTH: 384 B.C.

BIRTHPLACE: Stagirus, Macedonia

FATHER: Nicomachus

MOTHER: Phaestis

EDUCATION: Academy of Plato in Athens

SPOUSE: Pythias

DATE OF MARRIAGE: 347 B.C.

CHILDREN: Pythias

CHILD FROM OTHER RELATIONSHIP: Nicomachus

DATE OF DEATH: 322 B.C.

PLACE OF DEATH: Euboea, Greece

Further Reading

Anderson, Margaret J., and Karen F. Stephenson. *Aristotle: Philosopher and Scientist.* Berkeley Heights, N.J.: Enslow Publishers, 2004.

Anderson, Margaret J., and Karen F. Stephenson. *Scientists of the Ancient World.* Springfield, N.J.: Enslow Publishers, 1998.

Gay, Kathlyn. *Science in Ancient Greece.* London: Franklin Watts, 1999.

Hakim, Joy. *The Story of Science: Aristotle Leads the Way.* Washington: Smithsonian Books, 2004.

Nardo, Don. *Ancient Philosophers.* San Diego: Lucent Books, 2004.

Parker, Steve. *Aristotle and Scientific Thought.* New York: Chelsea House Publishers, 1995.

Look for more Signature Lives books about this era:

Alexander the Great: *World Conqueror*
ISBN 0-7565-1872-5

Socrates: *Ancient Greek in Search of Truth*
ISBN 0-7565-1874-1

Thucydides: *Ancient Greek Historian*
ISBN 0-7565-1875-X

On the Web

For more information on *Aristotle* use FactHound.

1. Go to *www.facthound.com*
2. Type in this book ID: 0756518733
3. Click on the *Fetch It* button.

FactHound will find the best Web sites for you.

Historic Sites

National Archaeological Museum of Athens
44 Patission St.
106 82 Athens
Attica, Greece
011-30-210-8217724
Greek art including sculpture, pottery, bronzes, and prehistoric items

The Metropolitan Museum of Art
1000 Fifth Ave.
New York, NY 10028
212/535-7710
Artifacts, statues, and literature from ancient Greece

B.C.
a Christian term meaning "before Christ" and referring to dates that occurred before the birth of Jesus; B.C. dates decrease as time goes on

cephalopods
a group of ocean-dwelling mollusks, including octopus and squid

democratic
relating to a government system run by officials elected by citizens

dialogues
a series of questions asked back and forth to stimulate thought

embryology
the study of how organisms develop

ethics
standards of behavior and moral judgment

hypotheses
scientific predictions about what will happen in an experiment

invertebrates
animals without backbones

logic
science of the formal principles of reasoning

metaphysics
the study of the nature of existence and how we know what we know

philosopher
a person who studies ideas, the way people think, and the search for knowledge

philosophy
the search for wisdom and knowledge

premises
statements that serve as the basis for an argument

rational
based on reason; able to reason

regent
a person appointed to rule in place of, or together
with, another

rhetoric
the art of speaking or writing effectively

syllogism
a deductive scheme of a formal argument consisting
of a major and minor premise and a conclusion

teleology
the belief that a natural object has a definite goal
and end purpose

Chapter 1
Page 13, line 1: Ben Waggoner. "Aristotle." 12 Dec. 2005. www.ucmp.berkeley.
edu/history/aristotle.html

Chapter 4
Page 33, line 19: Benjamin Farrington. *Aristotle: Founder of Scientific Philosophy*. New York: Praeger, 1969, pp. 24–25.
Page 35, line 26: Ibid., pp. 38–39.
Page 38, line 15: Robert Maynard Hutchins. *Great Books of the Ancient World: The Works of Aristotle*, Vol. 2. Chicago: Encyclopedia Britannica, 1952, p. 57.
Page 41, line 14: Ibid., p. 87.
Page 45, line 15: George Sarton. *A History of Science*, Vol. 1. Cambridge: Harvard University Press, 1952, p. 545.

Chapter 5
Page 50, line 24: Diogenes Laertius. *Lives of Eminent Philosophers*, Vol. 2. Cambridge: Harvard University Press, 1966, p. 459.
Page 51, line 7: Ibid., p. 457.

Chapter 6
Page 60, line 24: Robert Maynard Hutchins. *Great Books of the Ancient World: The Works of Aristotle*, Vol. 1. Chicago: Encyclopedia Britannica, 1952, p. 662.
Page 63, line 7: *Aristotle: Founder of Scientific Philosophy*, p. 66.
Page 67, line 7: Richard McKeon, ed. *The Basic Works of Aristotle.* New York: Random House, 1941, p. 66.
Page 68, line 3: Victor Katz. *A History of Mathematics: An Introduction.* Boston: Pearson Addison Wesley, 2004, p. 35.

Chapter 7
Page 72, line 13: *Aristotle: Founder of Scientific Philosophy*, p. 74.
Page 74, line 26: *Great Books of the Ancient World: The Works of Aristotle*, Vol. 1., p. 370.

Chapter 8
Page 79, line 14: *Aristotle: Founder of Scientific Philosophy*, p. 91.
Page 80, line 14: Ibid., p. 88.

Chapter 9
Page 86, line 1: *Lives of Eminent Philosophers*, Vol. 2., p. 445.

Downs, Robert B. *Landmarks in Science: Hippocrates to Carson.* Littleton, Colo.: Libraries Unlimited, Inc., 1982.

Farrington, Benjamin. *Aristotle: Founder of Scientific Philosophy.* New York: Praeger, 1969.

Katz, Victor J. *A History of Mathematics: An Introduction.* Boston: Pearson Addison Wesley, 2004.

Laertius, Diogenes. *Lives of Eminent Philosophers.* Vol. 2. Cambridge: Harvard University Press, 1966.

McKeon, Richard, ed. *The Basic Works of Aristotle.* New York: Random House, 1941.

Sarton, George. *A History of Science.* Vol. 1. Cambridge: Harvard University Press, 1952.

Waggoner, Ben. "Aristotle." 12 Dec. 2005. www.ucmp.berkeley.edu/history/aristotle.html

Sharon Katz Cooper is a writer and science educator. She enjoys writing about science and social studies topics for children and young adults. She lives in Fairfax, Virginia, with her husband, Jason, and son, Reuven.